Those Absences Now Closest

Books by Dzvinia Orlowsky

A Handful of Bees
Edge of House
Except for One Obscene Brushstroke
Convertible Night, Flurry of Stones
Silvertone
Bad Harvest
Those Absences Now Closest

Those Absences
Now Closest

Dzvinia Orlowsky

Carnegie Mellon University Press
Pittsburgh 2024

Acknowledgments

Grateful acknowledgment is made to the publications in which some of these poems first appeared, sometimes in different forms or with different titles:

AGNI: "Trembling, tucked into myself . . ."; *The American Poetry Review*: "Five Centos after Serhiy Zhadan, *What We Live For, What We Die For*"; *Bending Genres*: "3,000-Year-Old Trousers Found in Chinese Grave"; *BODY*: "Pitchfork: Ohio, 1978"; *CavanKerry Press* website: "By the time my refugee parents arrive at Ellis Island"; *Consequence Forum*: "Breaking News"; *Ethel Zine*: "Dog Girl's *Sick of* Song: Oxana Malaya," "At Night, When Everything Takes on Another Living Form"; *The Journal of the American Medical Association*: "Lullaby," "The Last Goodbye"; *Lily Poetry Review*: "Damaging Wind"; *Mom Egg Review*: "Newton's Cradle," "Our Dolls Were Naked"; *Nixes Mate Review*: "Night Rain"; *periodicities: a journal of poetry and poetics*: "Two Solitudes," "Prayer for the Heart," "War"; *Plume*: "The Village Crow," "If we weren't knocking on wood," "*Back in the U.S.S.R.*," "The Wind Cried Mary"; *Poetry Porch*: "Caprice," "Without Makeup," "To Winter"; *Pulse & Echo*: "Our Wagons Were Made Entirely out of Wood," "Whisperer"; *Solstice*: "Cento 6 after Serhiy Zhadan, *What We Live For, What We Die For*," "No Promise of Heaven"

"& Weep," appeared in *Lily Poetry Review: Voices Amidst the Virus: Poets Respond to the Pandemic*.

These poems were selected by Robert Pinsky for the New England Poetry Club's 2020 Samuel Washington Allen Prize for poem sequences: "Desolate," "Right Hand," "Measuring Grief," "Those Dogs Could Tell a Story," "Nightingales," "So Saints Can See," "Measuring for a Coffin," and "Scythes."

"9 Centos after Serhiy Zhadan, *What We Live For, What We Die For*" contains lines taken from *What We Live For, What We Die For: Selected Poems by Serhiy Zhadan* (Yale University Press, 2019) translated from the Ukrainian by Virlana Tkacz and Wanda Phipps, content used with permission from Yale.

With deep gratitude to Jay Hoffman for his love and encouragement in supporting the writing of this book. To Jeff Friedman, Candice Kelsey, Stuart Robbins for their close readings and generous comments. To Ernesto L. Abeytia, Thomas Thomas, and Joyce P. Wilson, for their keen feedback on individual poems. To Kathleen Aguero, Lisa Allen, Maria Luisa Arroyo, Genia Blum, Alan Britt, Barbara Siegel Carlson, Robert Carr, Eileen Cleary, Gabriel Cleveland, Jenifer DeBellis, Danielle De Tiberus, Lori DiPrete, Melanie Drane, Lee Hope, Meg Kearney, Daniel Lawless, Kirk Lawrence-Howard, Elizabeth Lund, Elizabeth Mercurio, Gloria Mindock, Maria Nazos, Anne-Marie Oomen, Miriam O'Neal, Catherine Sasanov, Neil Silberblatt, Joanna Solfrian, Elaine d'Entremont Sorrentino, Lisa Sullivan, Emily Van Duyne, Mark Walsh, Carolyne Lee Wright, my Solstice MFA in Creative Writing Program, *Solstice* literary magazine and Providence College families—dear friends, how you inspire.

Last but never least, all gratitude to Cynthia Lamb and Connie Amoroso for their generous help and attention in bringing this and other books out into the world. And especially to you, Gerald Costanzo, for 30 years of believing in my work.

Book design by Jen Bortner

for Doma Bonchuk

my maternal grandmother

&

for Jay, Max, Raisa, always

Contents

Prolog

11   "Trembling, tucked into myself, I recalled the Last Judgment."
Excerpt from The Enchanted Desna *by Oleksandr Dovzhenko*
Translated from the Ukrainian by Dzvinia Orlowsky

I.   The (Dis)enchanted Desna: A Poem Sequence

15   Desolate
17   Right Hand
18   Measuring Grief
19   Those Dogs Could Tell a Story
21   Nightingales
22   So Saints Can See
23   Measuring for a Coffin
25   Our Wagons Were Made Entirely out of Wood
26   The Village Crow
28   Scythes

Epilog

31   "Trembling, tucked into myself, I recalled the Last Judgment."
Erasure poem

II.   9 Centos after Serhiy Zhadan, *What We Live For, What We Die For*

35   Cento 1
36   Cento 2
37   Cento 3
38   Cento 4
39   Cento 5
40   Cento 6
41   Cento 7
42   Cento 8
43   Cento 9

III.

47   If we weren't knocking on wood

49   In the Burning

50   Pitchfork: Ohio, 1978

54   Newton's Cradle

56   Our Dolls Were Naked

58   *Back in the U.S.S.R.*

60   Dog Girl's *Sick of* Song: Oxana Malaya

61   Two Solitudes

62   Prayer for the Heart

63   Lullaby

65   No Promise of Heaven

67   To Winter

68   The Last Goodbye

70   Breaking News

72   War

76   & Weep,

IV.

79   At Night, When Everything Takes on Another Living Form

81   Caprice

83   Beets & Turnips & Kale

85   Without Makeup

87   Night Rain

89   Damaging Wind

90   3,000-Year-Old Trousers Found in Chinese Grave

92   Whisperer

93   The Wind Cried Mary

94   No Coming Back

Prolog

Trembling, tucked into myself, I recalled the Last Judgment. I looked up at the swallows and sighed. How helpless I was lying in Grandfather's boat and how schooled of unpleasant and bad things. How unpleasant it is when Grandmother curses at me or when long rain pelts down and doesn't want to stop. How unpleasant when a leech clings to your leg, or when strange dogs bark at you, or a goose hisses around your feet, nips at your pants with a red beak. And how unpleasant to carry with one hand a large bucket of water or to weed or tear off sideshoots of tobacco. How unpleasant when Father comes home drunk and fights with Grandfather, then with Mother, then throws plates. How unpleasant to walk barefoot over wheat stubs or to giggle in church when something strikes you as funny. Riding in a hay-filled wagon about to tip over is unpleasant. It's unpleasant to look at a large fire, but pleasant to look at its embers.

How pleasant it is to hug a foal. Or at daybreak to see your calf wandering in all by itself, to know it found its way home in the dark. How pleasant it is to wade in warm puddles after thunder or to catch a small pike with your bare hands, stir muddy water, or to watch someone slowly pull in a large net. How pleasant it is to find a bird's nest in the grass, to eat Easter buns and eggs. How pleasant when spring waters flood the house and everyone wanders all over, how pleasant to fall asleep in Grandfather's boat, in the fields of rye, millet, barley—and in all grains while they were drying on the oven. And of course, the smell of drying grain is pleasant. It's pleasant to drag a sheaf to a stack, to walk around the stacks, grain spilled everywhere. It's pleasant when an apple thought sour turns out to be sweet. It's pleasant when Grandfather yawns when bells ring out on a summer evening. It's also pleasant—and this I loved most—when Grandfather talked with a horse or foal as if they were human. I loved when out of the darkness on the road a voice called out, "Peace to you!" and Grandfather replied, "And may God grant you peace!"

I loved when a big fish tossed in the lake or in the purple stillness of the Desna at sunset. I loved to lie in a wagon, returning home from the meadow, to look up at the star-filled sky. I loved to drift off to sleep—when the wagon pulled around to the house and I was carried, asleep, inside. I loved the sound of wheels screeching under wagons heavy with harvest in August. Birds chirping in the garden and in the field. I loved swallows in barns, rails in meadows. I loved the splash of spring water. At twilight, the cry-croak of frogs during a rainfall in a bog. I loved the songs of girls—carols, songs of the New Year, the coming of spring, the harvest songs. I loved the thud of apples in the orchard at dusk when they fall unexpectedly into the grass. A certain mystery and sadness, the inevitability and law that out of what seemingly ends, come the pleasant things of this world.

I loved thunder, although it scared Mother, the downpour and loud wind for the gifts they brought to the orchard.

I

The (Dis)enchanted Desna: A Poem Sequence

—after Oleksandr Dovzhenko (1894-1956)
in a time of Putin

Desolate

He had no soul, only steam,
no eyes, only two frying pans,
no mouth, only a daub of red,
no throat, only a chimney
that choked him,
no God, only a candle
placed upside down.

He had no voice, only drones,
no skin, only a sheepskin turned
inside out, no feet, only puddles
in which dirt swirled,
no conscience, only pigeons
spying from above.
He had no will, only a cracked

watermelon—seeds
instead of memories—
no woods, only withered grass,
no roar, only labored horses
and buckling calves,
no bread, only one bowed fruitless tree.
He had no angels, only the din of buzzing bees.

He had no road to cross.
no country, only a stinging nettle,
no sins, only a thunder of artillery,

no soldiers, only tongues over fires.
no children, only graveside flowers,
no legs, though at times, they ran
like rivers of blood.

Right Hand

He held in his right hand
tender calves and dipped-back horses,

a devil escaped from a circus,
prowling on the riverbank.

With his right hand, he shut all dusky
windows and wind-blown doors,

commanded, with a vigorous gesture,
that a seventh son be born

while spinsters swept
all houses clean.

He forbid his left hand from interfering
with its menial work.

When he raised his right hand,
chickens burst out of their coops

only to collapse, their feathers
scattered among straw—

rabbits disappeared into tiny holes,
The orange sunset tore itself on black branches

but worshippers called it beautiful,
considered themselves saved.

Measuring Grief

First, unravel yards of sunlight
so that they reach stone corners
of darkest winter cottages.

Listen for snow's slow dripping
from thatched roofs. It'll sound
like intermittent tears—

a broken circle, a drumming,
bird song pause. It'll urge you,
head down, slope-shouldered,

to open the door. Cut the last
threads of light before you enter.
Let the air, instead,

carry the smell of dung,
the ashy dust of lampblack rising,
whitewashing its soul.

Those Dogs Could Tell a Story

Assessing everything around them,
gut fires burning, their masters
devoured by dreams,

each dog offered a different story—
some of great heroics, nipping at a soldier's
feet; others added a note of despair:

fleas bouncing to the tips of their tails,
water freezing in puddles—small
broken mirrors, omens of bad luck.

What about a little salt in our bowls?
What about hiring a guard for our food?
they growled among themselves.

Often, they'd wait until midnight
on the Feast of the Epiphany, the wisest
among them, elderly and large,

narrowing his eyes, lost in thought.
Who would dare break the focus
of a dog scenting the wind

for a catchy opening line? How about,
they agreed, starting with a master's praise:
good boy Valentyn, lovely lady Sophia,

clipped into surnames:
willow whip, splinter storm—
a morsel of dinner offered near the back door.

And never upon us, a drunken hand!
This made even the mice reel,
eavesdropping under the cupping boards.

Nightingales

Slipped into silence
neither their once highly regarded

melancholic songs nor tattered bags
filled with brown feathers

could be swapped back
for once-upon-a time wisdom—

Lacking purpose and star quality,
no one cared anymore if, trapped

in cages, they could sing
single sonorous notes

or if scorched, at dawn,
be served on toast.

*Who is crying now? Who
is beating the horse?*

Worrying too much,
they turned into flycatchers.

So Saints Can See

Cut yourself with a dull razor. Blood flows
like a tzar's crimson goatee, his flimsy physique.

Burn your thoughts in silvery plumes. Words
hiss in oak struck by lightning.

Admit you gave up praying in exchange for thicker smoke.
A pope's chasuble flares luscious tobacco leaves.

Hour to hour shadows dart low. Meadow birds
predict foul weather.

Ask for nothing more, get nothing less—
pike and pillows stuffed to the gills with straw.

Loudly strum a *bandura* without a plectrum. Offer up
fledgling flies, your pilfered breadcrumbs.

Measuring for a Coffin

Inside, find your great-grandmother
laid out on a bench, her head
pointed toward icons, her curses—

may your knees break—vanished
She will appear shorter
than you remember her.

Give her six feet. She'll take with her
a second helping of the last road
that stretched before her,

the early cock's crow—
just so you and your family won't
have it all.

Go the full 18 inches deep.
Remember her pelvis,
an emptied water trough,

her shoulders, heavy as two geese
struck by lightning,
her head, a bulbous melon

All these will have to fit.
And while you are working, whistle,
as if life were a song—

You'll want God to hear
that you are good, kind—charitable
with an extra inch or foot.

You'll want your pigs to think
they'll be fed well for the slaughter,
blind beggars to think you're rich.

Our Wagons Were Made Entirely out of Wood

Iron hubs attracted restless skies,
lightning strikes that split sin

from sinner, seedy chatter
from swampy gossip,

desolation from everyday sorrow's
slumping silhouettes—

they could make hair stand
on heads or arms,

but by then it was too late.
The angry rumbling called out

hungry, aggressive dogs with black leathery bodies,
scaly patches of fur,

who barked hoarsely behind each filled wagon
halted now and then by a hidden rock,

tiny avalanches of grain spilling
onto the dirt road.

Because breath was wasted on isolated,
lofty thoughts,

some wagoners chose to keep
the iron, the thunderheads'

pressed fists, rickety wheels
rutting the ground.

The Village Crow

The village crow knew everything—
whose son fathered young partisans,

guns like large broken wishbones
pressed to their chests,

which rooster crowed *get up!*
confusing death with daily rising—

which neighbor's
hatchet would outlive him,

Water is the enemy!
Some claimed the crow was older

than the oldest oak. Others swore
it was brought by the devil, one year,

to act as interpreter for blasphemers,
sleepwalkers, and arsonists.

No one cared about angels anymore.
The crow had special tricks.

Before a hunter lifted his rifle,
blasted the bird into a comet of feathers,

*it could bring down enough rain
to spoil the hay.* When it cawed,

the lake grew quiet,
clouds darkened the sky

covering the water's surface.
Fish presumed their days were numbered,

hiding among swampy drapes.
But even fishermen before casting their lines

removed their hats, cried out in disbelief:
Does anyone recognize me?

Scythes

No more sweeping sounds
reaping crops,

the heavy pendulum swing of bodies,
railroad tracks of shuffling feet.

No more field stubble,
prickly childhood steps—

Grandfather's unwinding songs
like long narrow strips of grass.

No more scythes
breaking into evening,

clouds bulking
against the sky—

hammered blades fading.
Listen and sleep.

Campfires release
their sluggish gunfire,

finches swap calls
for brambly thorns.

Epilog

Trembling, tucked into myself, I recalled the Last Judgment. I looked up at the swallows and sighed. How helpless I was lying in Grandfather's boat and how schooled of unpleasant and bad things. How unpleasant it is when Grandmother curses at me or when long **rain** pelts down and **doesn't** want to **stop**. How unpleasant when a leech clings to your leg, or when strange dogs bark at you, or a goose hisses around your feet, nips at your pants with a red beak. And how unpleasant to carry with one hand a large bucket of water or to weed or tear off side shoots of tobacco. How unpleasant when Father comes home drunk and fights with Grandfather, then with Mother, then throws plates. How unpleasant to walk barefoot over wheat stubs or to giggle in church when something strikes you as funny. Riding in a hay-filled wagon about to tip over is unpleasant. It's unpleasant to look at a large fire, but pleasant to look at its embers.

How pleasant it is to hug a foal. Or at daybreak to see your calf wandering in all by itself, **to know** it found its way home in the dark. How pleasant it is to wade in warm puddles after thunder or to catch a small pike with **your bare hands**, stir muddy water, or to watch someone slowly pull in a large net. How pleasant it is to find a bird's nest in the grass, to eat Easter buns and eggs. How pleasant when spring waters flood the house and everyone wanders all over, how pleasant to fall asleep in Grandfather's boat, in the fields of rye, millet, barley—and in all grains while they were drying on the oven. And of course, the smell of drying grain is pleasant. It's pleasant to drag a sheaf to a stack, **to walk around** the stacks, grain spilled everywhere. It's pleasant when an apple thought sour turns out to be sweet. It's pleasant when Grandfather yawns when bells ring out on a summer evening. It's also pleasant—and this I loved most—when Grandfather talked with a horse or foal as if they were human. I loved when out of **the darkness** on the road a voice called out, "Peace to you!" and Grandfather replied, "And may God grant you peace!"

I loved when a big fish tossed in the lake or in the purple stillness of the Desna at sunset. I loved **to lie** in a wagon, returning home from the meadow, to look up at the star-filled sky. I loved to drift off to sleep—when the wagon pulled around to the house and I was carried, asleep, inside. I loved the sound of wheels screeching under wagons **heavy with** harvest in August. Birds chirping in the garden and in the field. I loved swallows in barns, rails in meadows. I loved the splash of spring water. At twilight, the cry-croak of frogs during a rainfall in a bog. I loved the songs of girls—carols, songs of the New Year, the coming of spring, the harvest **songs.** I loved the thud of apples in the orchard at dusk when they fall unexpectedly into the grass. A certain mystery and sadness, the inevitability and law that out of what seemingly ends, come the pleasant things of this world.

I loved thunder, although it scared Mother, the downpour and loud wind for the gifts they brought to the orchard.

II

*Spring is not regulated and does
not get out of order*

—E.E. Cummings, "9."

9 Centos after Serhiy Zhadan, *What We Live For, What We Die For*

Cento 1

—based on opening lines by Serhiy Zhadan

Take only what is most important. Take the letters,
the dark shattered wicked winter.

You hear everything passing,
stories connected with murders, knife wounds.

Remember how winter began in your town.
The hot heart of the year is burning.

Where are you coming from, dark caravan, you flock of birds?
You will reply today touching the warm letters.

Cento 2

—based on eighth lines by Serhiy Zhadan

Blown-up bodies.
In times of peace, they were just considered members of a sect.

Now we smell the burning even in our dreams.
Take the letters, all of them, every last piece of bad news

reminds you
they were led out at night their dreams scattering.

So what difference does it make what I crawl past?
No one will return from the long night walks.

Cento 3

—based on ninth lines by Serhiy Zhadan

Churches and train stations are heated only by long conversations—
hearths of home heated by the breath of entire provinces.

Every night used to flow by slowly, like a river,
ran between your fingers till you woke up.

What will survive from the history
of the Lord's commandments? Deaf and angry,

what did you want?
You will pass through that mercurial time between seasons

and snails will die forgotten on the wet grass.
I will remember the sky and how high it seemed.

What did you want?

Cento 4

—based on twentieth lines by Serhiy Zhadan

angels wings on the submissive surface of the world
which people constantly borrowed,

and all these preachers on lifeguard towers—
everyone can find something if they only look carefully.

No green valleys, no suburban wastelands—
you will stand like a ghost in the fog, gold scattered about.

In the noise and the headlights,
our unspoken conversations, unseen heavens.

Every sin is like a stone from the seashore
that forces you to love

and now dreams break off
and you inhale.

Writing into the void
is like the love of trees that grow without you.

There's nothing but sky
the workers took home.

Tell us anything that's not on the news.

Cento 5

—based on closing lines by Serhiy Zhadan

Let their journey be easy, let them be rescued in time
under the burning sky.

And really—it is nothing,
the smell of corpses

will say there's no reason to write about this at all.

The cities freeze in the night—
stars

around your heart.
Fly into its light.

No one will be too late.

Cento 6

—based on second lines by Serhiy Zhadan

Silence waits at the door like death.

See the fading red paint blistering on the window frames,

how everyone who dared to stay and live
forged—link by link—

suicides, botched abortions—in general . . .

There are no candies in the lobby or in the rooms—of course—
so you need to know where you're going.

. . . Sorting through them in the dark, confusing consonants with vowels,

you hear everything remaining.

Cento 7

When Easter arrives, the sky becomes kinder
with the post office in the slow thaw.

Get out of the rainy street and into the auditorium.
Suddenly it feels like there's a lot of water.

I searched for her for a long time. She changed her number,
bad family history,

Sasha, a quiet drunk, an esoteric, a poet
Ihor, a chaplain, thirty years old.

"He's sorry for the city," he says. "It will be destroyed."
The cellist drags—

This happened some fifteen years ago, if I'm not mistaken.

Slow summer, endless, and some days are young.
So I throw down my weapon and start to crawl.

Cento 8

—based on thirteenth lines by Serhiy Zhadan

They were afraid, didn't understand, left town.
Then some of them returned.

Cigarette butts fall on the wet grass—
like contraband.

Gravestones will tell our stories best.
The dead speak under the earth, the saints from the heavens above.

There are two paths, lightly bouncing.
But the sky grows heavier every autumn.

The moon manages to move from the street corner closer to the church
and new jazz, which was supposed to be revived by white folks and
    other nonsense.

We will run past fields of sunflowers
to end up watching life from the windows of the bus stations.

Remember the snow of your lashes.

Cento 9

—based on other closing lines by Serhiy Zhadan

The earth under tired feet,

pills that don't exist,
just as there is no death.

You must realize how unlucky we've all been
in this barrack

like lost toys.
Check them for your own name

and then cross them out
as only you can.

Not too bad, I guess, for a city of over a million,
of music start to seed

in the damned ice,
in memory of all the dead.

Strange—strange, fantastic world.
This is what stops them . . .

with its heart.

III

You, congregation
of one

are here to listen
not to sing.

Kneel in the back pew.
Make no sound,

let the candles
speak.

—Patricia McKernon Runkle,
"When You Meet Someone Deep in Grief"

If we weren't knocking on wood

or spitting our way to safety, we
were always busy looking for signs
from our deceased loved ones
who still cared enough to visit.

A branch hanging crooked meant
a missed connection. We developed
a mystical lexicon for our secret beliefs.
"Unfounded" implied: *A stronger signal*

from the afterlife is yet to come.
"Groundless" confirmed: *Look to the sky.*
The dead always had our best interest
in mind. All we had to do was ask.

My mother died on August 30, the same
as my father, surviving him by 29 years.
One night, recognizing her imminent death,
my sister and I prayed to him to come

and escort her into the next world.
My father was a resilient, good-natured man.
And he played the guitar. Maybe my mother
remembered his body as song.

He would settle in outside her window
and chirp, wings raised and rubbing. But
I never understood why a frog; there was
something in that appropriation—

imagining his eager thumping forward
in the grass—that made him seem

excessively soft and vulnerable.
I don't know how he appeared to her

the night she died. Or what transported
him to her bedside. Most likely, it wasn't
a Carriage—or something fragile as a cricket—
more likely a bird, or just a feather.

We looked around on the floor
and found nothing. But we knew
his heart was in it—by the way
the phone rang three times then stopped.

In the Burning

But who would choose to be whipped with fire?

Unless in the burning there can be great light,
Unless the lightning that strikes terror
Lights enough to show the boundaries
Where terror ends
And at the limits, still enduring and alive,
Shows me myself
And a hope no longer blind.

(Meditation, Gates of Repentance)

By the time my refugee parents arrive at Ellis Island in 1950, relocate to Pleasant City, southern Ohio in 1951, they are children again. They surround themselves with 10 acres of meadow, seven dogs, three cats, two birds, one horse and eventually, two daughters, promising peace. Each Fourth of July, my father plants a celebratory sparkler into dirt dazzled by its blaze; he watches it sizzle and smoke into nothingness. We survived the war—he reminds himself—lightening doesn't strike twice. Each Fourth of July, my father years dead from cancer, my mother, trembling, waves us away. Outside fireworks hiss and spin. The sky opens up into a fly zone.

Pitchfork: Ohio, 1978

1.

I don't remember grabbing it
from our barn
           that morning
three malpractice lawyers
stood in our driveway,
wrapping up my father's
claim:

           the X-ray unchecked,
the cancer spread, rampant
as wildfire

How to move water to those fires?—
drop by drop
from puddles
to waking life

2.

I welcome the unexpected—

how farm tools take on a different life
hanging inside a barn,
less useful, untouched,

yet inside our home:
long handle, five curved tines

legal jargon pitched
toward Father's

incoherence,
the deposition
that like an already full glass
would never hold

low listless hum of work,
proof that the dying are still
with us

3.

Raised to be polite,
I offered each lawyer
tiny sweets, iced
water with a bitter twist,
until the heat
in my parents' bedroom
gave off a cloying smell—

What year did you finish your residency?
He couldn't answer
Poland or Ukraine?
He couldn't answer questions of place
When did you come to America? But
holding up a ski trophy
he kept near his bed,
hand shaking, voice shaking
then crying, he responded . . . *1978*
as if recalling a favorite song
with sound mind

For three months, my mother stood up,
left his room to let the dogs out
One day, a letter arrived

4.

The deposition held up in court
Father already passed,
compensated for work hours
lost

I don't remember grabbing it
from our barn that morning
three malpractice lawyers
stood in our driveway

or thanking them
for making
the drive out—

5.

P.S. one wrote on the letter:

What a treat, so pretty
in your green farm dress,
a pitchfork raised, ready to drive
it through each one of us,
"Get off our property!"

Farm tools take on a different life
hanging inside a barn—
less useful, untouched,

I don't remember grabbing it
Just a girl, untouched,
barefoot on the gravel

Newton's Cradle

—Fourth of July

1.

A crazy good time for everyone drinking
and blowing themselves up,

for the guns, bells, and the bonfires,
and for the flames hurled towards the tops of buildings.

But not for our dog, Petroushka,
swaddled in an old nightgown, shaking.

Not for my mother anxiously rocking her,
pillows propping her up in bed.

Not for silence
beating with an animal heart, the synchronized

clockwork held within a small rib cage,
short-haired fur—as soft, she used to say,

as a velvet glove lost behind
an opera house seat

or dropped in the snow searching for a key.
A luxury one couldn't count on.

2.

Not for the sky backfiring into showering
white spiders, the dog's pupils

darkening into small black umbrellas.
Not for bad luck getting personal in July 1942.

Not for the unwanted child aborted on a kitchen table.
Who would take care of it—

An unborn brother
or sister blocking Mother's ears

with ghostly small fingers.
Not for birds that lie scattered lifeless on the ground

or for the disoriented bees that won't go back to their hives.
Stars & Stripes Forever rushing to its end.

3.

Not for her waving me away: *Leave me alone.*
Or calling me back: *Stay if you understand.*

I wish I'd stayed. I kissed
the top of her head and left.

Some skies are impermeable to fire.
Some fires die as red skies.

Like silver slingshot balls, the collisions
would resound forever.

Our Dolls Were Naked

Our dolls were naked, but our cats stayed
partly clothed—a ribbon here, a brown felt hat there,
two holes cut and fitted for their ears.

My sister and I wanted them pretty
for when the priest came to dinner.
They'd mew in the hallway, plunk heavy

onto their sides. We waited for the priest
to remove his hat, smile, extend his cool hand
to touch our faces in approval

like Christ to his believers. Instead
he murmured that we were cruel,
headed straight for hell.

My sister's baby doll was large, shiny, round-faced.
Mine was narrow, loose-limbed, rubbery.
It peed rust when I squeezed its belly.

The cats clawed, scratched, refused to be babies.
Like all bad mothers, we grew sharper teeth,
longer noses and learned how to change

the color of our eyes. Frightened of us,
our dolls suffered from stomachaches,
lay prone on the brick walkway

until we took them to the faceless doctor
who administered lilac water jabs
to the soles of their feet.

Shushing them, we brushed invisible
strands of hair from their faces.
The cats rarely got sick.

Lifting them by the armpits,
we reassured them they had enough heft
to eclipse the sun—

The cats celebrated their nine lives.
We worried that they'd stop needing us.
And how we missed hugging our dolls!

But the dolls, too, wanted no part of us—
playing hide-and-seek in every darkened room
we couldn't even imagine.

Back in the U.S.S.R.

—Lennon-McCartney

1.

We weren't the Beach Boys' California girls,
weren't *the cutest in the world*, no French bikinis
cut to fit our McDonald's and Coca-Cola
bodies. We bit eyes and a mouth into bologna
slices, lay the cool-skin masks
against our faces, sprayed Sun-In on

our ash blond hair until it streaked bright
yellow—a signature look—free, almost
graffitied, like yellow snow. Once, I surfed
Lake Erie to my sister's cheers, stood up
on a rental board, balancing for a minute,
the tiny wave beneath me lifting and curling

just long enough to make it count—though
I'm not sure what for. O Maria, Chris, Nuni, Natalie—
even our theme park tissue *Flower Power*
blooms held seductively against our hips, O
steamy dance halls in the dark never
sparked a glance from any boy.

2.

We swore we'd end up marrying each other,
exchange vows with dyed *good luck*
rabbits' feet, key chains for keys we'd most
likely never own, doors that opened
to beauty queens who waved from county
fair floats pulled by tractors.

Then Paul McCartney sang it:
The Ukraine girls really knock me out!
What? *They leave the West behind.*
Really? *Back in the U.S.S.R.* The U.S.S.R.
Our popularity was sealed.
We began waiting by our phones.

3.

We didn't appreciate irony back then—
Come and keep your comrades warm
My father's heated "Over my dead body!"
Let me hear your balalaika's ringing out!
"No patriotic Ukrainian plays
a Russian balalaika!"

But the Ukraine girls knocked *somebody* out—
Soon we, too, would be called to ecstasy's
snow-peaked mountains.
Honey, disconnect the phones.
How exciting, at night, to rub bright
purple rabbit fur against our faces,

gently press to our lips
the tips of crescent nails.
We wallowed in the luck we believed
they'd continue to bring—
Useless Sad Saturated Relics
dangling from small chains.

Dog Girl's *Sick of* Song: Oxana Malaya

—after Sylvia Plath's "Mad Girl's Love Song"

I was born a real girl but came to light as dog instead.
They barked. I answered. Left outside: 3 years old, I still couldn't speak.
(My parents thought me a weary load / my parents wanted me dead.)

I slept on a kennel floor, learned to howl to be fed.
I scavenged rubbish tossed to dirt, refined tearing meat.
I was born a real girl, grew up dog instead.

Surrounded by bitches—my renown was bred!
They taught me to lick myself clean.
(My parents thought me a weary load / my parents wanted me dead.)

Matu i *Bat'ko*, shit-drunks, played to the frayed thread.
Twenty-two years later they refuse to be seen.
I was born a real girl but grew up dog instead.

Does abandoned make us less human, toward what god are we bled?
Wild child mongrel, I've learned no one to please,
(My parents thought me a weary load / my parents wanted me dead.)

I have no use for mirrors, a feral heart needs no feather bed.
Tell me I'm family, shock me into your dream.
Born a girl, lived dog, became a woman instead.
(I carry no weary load / my parents are dead.)

Two Solitudes

My grandmother named me *poor orphan*,
the one her daughter could no longer carry,

delivered weeks early into her arms.
Keeper of birds with damaged wings,

of pecked sunflowers. She made up songs
that made her cry. Other times,

she called me *dzvinyochka,* palest blue
bell-shaped flower. But when she pressed

her head against mine, she heard
nothing. Yet *nothing* drew static winter skies

instead of the drifting promises
of lullabies—diamond-stars,

bands of angels, three bags full.
I wasn't her son, whom she believed

still called out for her, twenty years on,
from a ghost-occupied Siberian labor camp.

Was it me she loved, me she held?
Or those absences

now closest to him.

Prayer for the Heart

As long as bombs don't drop on those
    who've fled,

as long as one spare god still hovers
    above their beds.

As long as cattle cars roll forward
    and do not stop,

as long as Grandmother's large
    ceramic vase

doesn't drop from her hands
    at the train station.

Why did she refuse to leave it behind
    holding everyone up,

splitting the family
    in two—?

Those who boarded & those who stayed
    to gather the pieces,

fit them back together—
    disappearing in clouds of steam.

What holds us
    to the colorless burn

of family—
    who *wake in another skin*, unhealed.

Lullaby

I sang to it, turning the key
on the small white lace musical pillow
given at birth to my son
by a man now dust.
Its quivering mechanical pitches
pulsed against the bruised skin,
the deepening twilight yellow
from the biopsy needle. No longer
afraid, my fingers glided over
its smooth globe, vacant ballroom,
mirrors draped and crackled.
If I loved it, maybe it would leave me.
I held it, honed tiger steps,
red velvet walls of the heart,
paws large enough to carry us
through any cold room, hips swaying
like a pendulum, lugubrious tail
trailing the polished floor,
chairs knocked over. Other nights,

I dreamed the earth opened her eyes,
took us both into her long dirt corridors,
and wondered if winter's trees
would satisfy all the seeds
it hungered for, set with shadows,
a table offering water—
I tried to love it, confused it with a child.
It was part of me; went everywhere I went.
I saw the pity in the eyes of neighbors.
I spoke of this pity to no one.
All winter, I ate only what had skin—
black threads, pocked,

orange, the citrus split into glass,
tiny orange flecks.

Why shouldn't I sing?
Silence gathered into a bowl.
Nothing had turned it away.
It found home in the rain and stayed.
Warm and safe, it stretched forward,
turned and curled into my song.

No Promise of Heaven

—after Hieronymus Bosch's Death and the Miser

1.

No promise of heaven, endless pink ribbon woven
Between slats of white
Picket fence; an offering of a potted geranium,
Drooping leaves, absent stem,
Small *get-well* card tied to its node. Neighbor, I saw you
Peeking through my window, afraid to knock, before you
Drove away, before I could thank
You, turn my eyes from gray
Back to blue. Before I could ask you to stay. No
Angel's hand on my left
Shoulder to steady me, no crucifix
Suspended like a tailless kite
High in the window—just death bride-white offers of
Radiation, lance-like paintbrush pointing at cells on the tip
Of a pin. I took the sun and fed it my fear.
I drank red wine as if
It was water. O! I danced, partnerless,
Called it lying still.

2.

Forgive me my transparencies, X-rays,
Scarred asymmetry, skin to bone, a sword driven
Through my wooden frame, the locked pirated chest
Where I hid dropped coils of hair. I tried not to
Think about letting the rest go: my eyebrows
And lashes—no red-skirted helmet
To protect my face. I prayed not
To forfeit what I thought was mine. Why

These star-starved mornings,
Bald demons chuckling as they roll
Out of my bed? No one would
Guess this to be a marriage—their prodding,
My hoarding—decades of rosary beads.
But what, yet unnamed, is left to count on?
My body turned toward brightest light?
Will I be willing to give up the extras of last moments—
The warm unknowing, pink drapes of rain,
My palm forced open.

To Winter

Love passes from prayer
To a light rainfall, each drop anchorless

And nameless. Where are the saints
Of wild grass, the ones I believed I could

Find if I brushed my hand through
Their green? I walk across the taut spaces

That thread my rosary,
Bead after hard bead,

The repeated lavender lifted to my lips,
Grateful for such moments

When blood blossoms under the sun,
And sorrow finds its shade.

Language of cold air, blank canvas of distance,
Who's keeping count?

The Last Goodbye

erupted from my father's mouth
in a thin stream of blood,
his body slumping forward against my shoulder,
almost lifting like a jockey relieving
his horse of his weight.

It held no regrets—no
I'm sorry to leave this way.
Instead, it emptied the last cup of bedside water,
hurried us to change his night shirt,
left us hanging in heavy, dried-up sleep.

Mornings, I'd swear:
There's sun on his face!
His flint blue eyes sparked!

Evenings, I'd administer the drugs,
slide a shot of morphine into muscle,
my hands shaking, interfering—
his body already a locked room.

Where were my loose, invisible reins
that would let him guide me,
promise nothing?
This isn't what we prayed for—
a shock of red silk
pulled through brambles.

If hearing is the last sense to go,
did he hear the sky grow quiet?

No remorse.
God is good—
like holding two baby birds in your hands.

Breaking News

1.

What breaks one person
   revives another

What breaks into silence
   breaks through to eternity

But what if heaven is bombed
   & clouds

no longer diaphanous
   split like dried earth

crumble into dust, mortal
   as family

2.

What war?
   The soil is well drained

for peonies whose only passion
   is to be unforgettable red

the hummingbird moth wishes for clover
   the skin on your ankle

for a blade of grass
   to sweep against it

What war?
      The sky has plenty of room

Petitions buzz like bees
      or lift into kites

if you run fast enough
      pull hard against the winds

Seven months in
      no one reports the bombings anymore

What war?
      (silence—imagine that)

3.

Imagine three birds at night
      calling out to their mates

I made it! I'm still here!
      In the meantime, a woman lies

trapped under the rubble
      of a nine-story building. Everyone's

praying she's still alive
      Prayer is *hope*

But what is hope, other than guess work
      & guesswork is

the surefire way not to get to heaven

War

How many deaths must it take to be considered a war?
—1,000 lives, Google

But the first 100 are only fooling.
They've saved their caboodles from drama class.
Death makeup is a breeze.

They clear their throats, step into the spotlight, center stage.

A mother applauds.
Outside, moonlight carves its solid world.

* * *

The second 100 are children again.

They run through fields of daisies,
fingers interlocked, index fingers pointing.

Ra-ta-tat-tat!

We're safe!

Migrative imagination,
pretend machine guns

execute a pact.

* * *

The third 100 drag their feet, lost,
heavy with song.

Song is healthy for the soul.
But who will listen?

Fearful neighbors
slam their doors shut.

Surely you understand, they whisper.

* * *

The fourth 100 never vacate their apartments.

They're still there
lying quiet in their beds,

their bodies packed with prayers.

A concrete city block disintegrates
between earth and air.

* * *

The fifth 100 simply refuse to die

until they find their daughters'
favorite stuffed bear,

the one with the black-button, blind eyes

that keeps her safe at night.

* * *

The sixth 100 press their ears to a hollow wall.

Who is shouting in the dark?
Not everyone who hears voices is unwell.

* * *

A plastic View-Master, a last luxury to be held
in their son's hands,

the seventh 100 cry a creek—a stream—a river

* * *

The eighth 100

don't remember first words,
don't hear last screams—

          their mouths open like that of a toddler
                gasping for air.

* * *

A living heart!

    Here!

The ninth 100 believe they are still
warm inside,

the way a burning forest believes
it's a perfect metaphor for the spiritual world

even after it's ash.

* * *

999

. . . are missing one
      who got away.

Praise be!

& Weep,

—after Anne Waldman's "& Sleep, the Lazy Owl of Night"

& Weep, the blossoming drifts of blight

& Weep, the toxic tips of tongues

& Weep, the infected and the arrested—the dead

& Weep, the songs of sirens under distancing clouds

& Weep, the reedy fringes of breath

& Weep, the cold stone, an attendant's gossamer scrubs

& Weep, the burning eye held open

& Weep, the heart that bursts in the throat

IV

Let the stones tell it.
Let the river sing it again.
Listen closely to the silence.
Listen to a language
not our own.

—Sam Hamill, *Habitation*

At Night, When Everything Takes on Another Living Form

This intuition was most apparent after sundown when you
gazed into their large, gray horse-eyes
—*Oleksandr Dovzhenko*

—*for WL (1945-2015)*

Ask the horse if it knows

        that night-dew can hurt
        the drying hay bale when the sun's first light
        snaps and spoils the fodder

        that its hair thickens with winter fringe

        that last letters never reach us

Ask the horse if it knows

        to what peace your body rushed off

        after the catastrophic fire
        On Amtrak's snow-covered tracks—
        a black tarry mark
        half the length of the first car
        Burned beyond recognition

        A different kind of ash

Ask the horse, the one that follows you to the blank page, if it knows

that as it inhales then
exhales, its nostrils
flare like poppies

that we're held for a moment
before the sky dissolves us

Caprice

1.

Approach a piano slowly as if it is a horse. Ease off the padded cover so as
not to startle or scratch beyond its initial shudder to the one small tug.

Lift the fallboard, open your music.

2.

If your imagination fails the horse, try meditating on milk poured from a
slightly lipped pitcher, pooling into your body thick as blood.

3.

Stand at a precipice. Listen to what sudden swarms of musical notes have
routinely warned you:

Sometimes a melody line snaps   like a pencil   Other times, like fireflies it
                                          appears
        out of nowhere   If you pedal Schubert   too much, he will
                sound   melted . . .

4.

Failing the hooves, the short pulses, the milk souring on your breath,
close your eyes. Try instead a variation:

Approach a piano slowly as you would a lover. Ease off the heavy cover to
expose long curves.

5.

Admit it: you are not a pianist.

Try not to flinch as the droves in sharps and flats recede to their hives.

Your imagined lover greets you in silence,

the room's clock duets with its mechanical hands.

Beets & Turnips & Kale

Thick coat of dust on the lid,
Gold's Borscht *best used by 2020*,

two years gone, moved from discount
to the international aisle

then back to discount—sad neighbor
of matzahs and buckwheat.

I'll tell my guests it's holy
which means served on starched

white linen embroidered with *JJH,*
my husband's initials. Like a prayer

off-limits to hunger, an animal
tired of its own blood, it'll stain the cloth.

The tail end of leftover soup
will disappear down the drain,

leave no trace for another year.
The teen boy cashier avoids my eyes,

Who eats this stuff . . . ?
Turnips roll on the conveyor belt

like heads of wrinkled, bearded old men.
Could easily be for my former husband or past lovers.

The boy doesn't bother to ask
what the fresh bunch of kale

is used for. *Beats me*—he rings it up
as Christmas decoration.

Without Makeup

—for my sister

I didn't know your late-in-the-day eyes,
cool, easy, calm lake of tired eyes.
You would say a *nothing green.*
Nothing anyone would notice.

I'd never know you hadn't slept—
face as bland as a manila folder
without the smoke blue pencil
drawn along your lower lids,

silver pewter smudges
running like paths of winter rain.
I didn't know your eyes set
the dinner table, made the bread rise,
turned violets into jelly.
I didn't know your eyes had candles.

Maria, we are the only two
left of our first family—
our parents now streaks
of bygone stories
even our mother's brightest
shade of tangerine lipstick
can't bring back.

Something has washed the mascara away,
Vaseline-rubbed your lashes.
You call it tired, unmotivated, grouchy looking,
apologize for apologizing,
I'm just beginning to see—

spring grass under snow
deciding which green.

Night Rain

I'd thought Grandmother was a delicate type, a fragrant phantom who floated into my room every night to check my breath. Not a woman who smoked and religiously watched *Friday Night Fights*.

Pearly clouds filled the living room, surrounded her. She dragged her Camel cigarette, tapped ashes into a drinking glass. On the TV, a rowdy crowd cheered. Three bells concluded the end of a round.

* * *

One man strikes a lucky blow, the other falls down. Who doesn't love a man who gives himself up? More than amateur boxing, she favored visits with priests. One brought kielbasa and vodka. His forgiving eyes said sin was like rain, both absolved in nature.

In the next room, my grandmother brought her own nature. She folded her apron, a rosary coiled into a tiny snake in one of its pockets, crossed the straps, patted her hair. She unfastened one glass button—a black ladybug nested high between the leaf spreads of her collar.

* * *

Just before her death, Grandmother dropped like a felled tree onto the floor of our living room. I woke to my mother's screams, to a dream of our house burning. Attendants guided her covered body on a stretcher. At the cemetery, my father said *be very quiet; having missed you so much, hearing your voices might just kill her again.*

* * *

She'd insisted grandchildren's voices were of an angelic choir; the silent ones needed the most cradling. Was I one of the angelic, one of the more silent ones? Sad music crackled through the funeral home speakers like fire.

Never again did God bleed summer rain, offer me nights of sunset-stain. Song swapped for a straight-to-the-back-of-the-throat shot of vodka, a mute peal of lavender pebble-shaped rosary beads. Asked *who, in the end, wins?* No one answered. A bell didn't ding. Tobacco dried up, left the ring.

Damaging Wind

Wind hid in the forest. Seasons came and went, but there were
no signs of devastated towns—no boarded restaurant windows or
collapsed porches. No chimes tinkling in the breeze. Some suspected
the wind herself was damaged.

Wind's father had been a boozy hurricane; her mother, a heated
argument between lovers in a cold motel room. But what was her
calling card? An overturned flowerpot, a torn kite lying in tall grass,
pages rustling in an open, unread book?

Occasionally a shingle flapped on a neglected barn roof, or a heavy
damp branch dropped on a neighbor plucking lawn mushrooms after
days of rain. But no one stood outside and said *the wind is going to be
nasty tonight.* No one replied *tell it to the wind.*

* * *

Nearly forgotten, Wind considered staging a comeback. She could
ruin a birthday party with flying debris or chase off the clowns who
were trying to take over the neighborhood. She could even make them
tumble. She could slap power lines onto asphalt roads, though pushing
a car off the road often left her gasping.

Hoping to gain more visibility, she tweeted a picture of herself as a
fully erect wind sock. This got her three followers. *You're the butt of
all jokes*, the leaves rustled. *You're just a flash of color*, Wind muttered
defensively. *Then a crumbled bit of nothing.*

Shamed, Wind mimicked dog whistles. Silenced, she became a shot of
rum, a blown over kiss, a mouth puckered in the hot, still air.

3,000-Year-Old Trousers Found in Chinese Grave

1.

So archeologists found the pants?
No bones about it.

In his low-hanging crotch pants, her
warrior could get her to do anything.
She'd neigh and nuzzle like a heavenly

steed, bend and flex in shadow dance
along their mud brick courtyard wall.
He'd whisper, "two branches" and point

to a moon drowned in olive oil
or to two roots of ginger and she'd
know he craved her shapely pale legs.

Kneeling before him, she'd run one hand
down his string belt and pull him closer
with the other.

2.

Suppose there was no battle, and the warrior
didn't saddle his squat, barrel-chested horse.
Then he would gladly trade it in for a kilo of tea.

Suppose he dreamed of mountains dissolving
into mist, a waterfall spilling out of the clouds.
Mesmerized by the seductive possibilities

of nothingness, he didn't notice the scorpion
scaling up his thigh, just past the cross-stitching,
midknee. The wide crotch didn't help. His pants

were a canvas on which the enemy's blood
would have painted many moments of greatness.
Instead, they pinned him to his death.

3.

Three thousand years later, the woman,
still faithful, untouched, turned into
a song whose lyrics were long forgotten.

The warrior, dusty, carbon dated
to middle age, died in his prime
under a moon wrapped in silk thread.

He left nothing foreign behind, no
petrified familial tongues or broken
prophetic black pottery shards

or wilted flowers to the heart—
just the trousers, threadbare,
disintegrating.

Whisperer

Lately, the whisperer found himself sleeping alone. His dog wouldn't share
the bed. He preferred to sleep on the stairs or on the buckling futon.

The dog stopped greeting him when he came home after work. *Back so soon?*
The squeaking donut once offered as prey gathered dust on the kitchen floor.

The more the dog whisperer brushed his dog, the more the dog seemed to
disappear. Thick wads pulled from the metal-toothed FURminator lined
like tumbleweeds long the kitchen counter.

I could stuff my pillow with it or use it to make a loose-knit sweater.
When the dog's stomach gurgled, the whisperer heard laughter.

I've lost my touch, the man whispered to himself. *This isn't much of a pack.*
He'd imagined a half-dozen trained rescues jumping through Hula Hoops.

He couldn't focus on the editorial he was writing; he burned his coffee. The
dog leaned against the wall, watching.

I'm not a leader, the man realized. *He's here because I'm his last hope for a meal,
nothing more.* The dog's eyes stared into him.

It's never as complicated as it seems.
Love's just one more thing worth learning a trick for.

The Wind Cried Mary

When Hendrix coaxed, *Are you experienced?*
      we answered *oh, quite contrary.*

Only wild meadow grass jazzed in evening light
      and the wind cried *Mary.*

Fringed backpacks, hair free flying, little lambs sure to go,
      we left the Midwest,

rake-thin, obsessed, to follow the lovesick wind
      crying *Mary.*

Who waters your green? A woman's nothing
      without a man!

The ocean heaved—*go!*
      but the wind cried *Marry.*

We picked up brooms *drearily sweeping,* Jacks-in-boxes
      we thought worth keeping.

How do we seem? we asked weeping;
      the wind waxed . . . *Merry.*

Our bodies gave them their heft, shape of their songs,
      —sweet Jesus, Joseph, and Mary—

why didn't we leave?

No Coming Back

Like a strong wind, Frank took to knocking nests out of trees. They were always empty, and he was damned if he'd let them forewarn the day he'd find himself living alone. And she was damned if she wasn't already saying goodbye, always in a long terry robe, her hair coiled and pinned tight on her head like some second-chance Amish bride. He wished she'd wear those tight faded jeans and crocheted bikini tops he'd found in a bag, scavenging around the clothes donation bin. She could tell by the way he stared at her as she washed her face that he imagined his hands pulling out those bobby pins, tousling her hair. *So damned ungrateful. . . .*

* * *

One morning, Frank dragged a large, wooden custom-built doghouse bought from a feedstore down the narrow driveway into the backyard. It was big enough to accommodate two 60-pound dogs. He wanted her close enough to feel her breath on his neck. He would tuck a small sleeping bag against the walls, pin her body against his. *What's this?* she asked. *Really, you have to ask?* he snapped. The surrounding chain-link fence—he could lock her in anytime, day or night. He threatened that if she ever left him there would be no coming back.

* * *

But she returned to place the divorce papers in the mailbox. Clumps of empty nests cluttered the backyard like hidden missiles among black branches. Above, she could see wisps of shapeless clouds mock her failed marriage. As she stood in the driveway, a few stray pieces of trash tumbled away from her. The tidy small house looked pretty in winter daylight, its flat roof glistening with snow. She had to give him that. She imagined him tucked inside, warm moist air turning to cold, refusing to come out. She'd be damned if he hadn't overlooked getting a door flap.

NOTES

Oleksandr (Alexander) Dovzhenko (1894–1956) was a Ukrainian literary stylist and filmmaker. The opening prose poem "Trembling, tucked into myself" is excerpted from his autobiographical novella, *The Enchanted Desna*, and translated from the original Ukrainian by me. The erasure poem and the poem sequence "The (Dis) Enchanted Desna, after Oleksandr Dovzhenko" are responses to this novella.

Desna is a major left tributary of the Dnieper River running through Russia and Ukraine. In Old East Slavic language, it means "right hand."

These centos are derived from *What We Live For, What We Die For: Selected Poems by Serhiy Zhadan* (Yale University Press, 2019) translated from the Ukrainian by Virlana Tkacz and Wanda Phipps, lines used with permission from Yale. The author's words and lines are retained as they appear in the original translations. Only the punctuation, in some places, has been modified.

Serhiy Zhadan (b. 1974) is a Ukrainian poet, novelist, essayist, musician, translator, and social activist. He has published 12 books of poetry and 7 novels, and winner of more than a dozen literary awards.

Oxana Malaya (b. 1983) is a Ukrainian woman internationally known as a feral child raised by dogs.

"Two Solitudes," "War," "Breaking News," and "Prayer for the Heart" are poems inspired by paintings by Romanian visual artist, Oana Maria Cajal, featured in the 2022–2023 international collaborative exhibition, *Shattered: Symbolic Gesture,* in solidarity with Ukraine. In "Prayer for the Heart" the words "wake in another skin" are taken from Dennis Schmitz's "Bathing in Dead Man Creek."

"3,000-Year-Old Trousers Found in Chinese Grave" is inspired by woolen pants found in 2014 in a grave in Yanghai, China's Xinjiang region. The fabric was carbon-dated to sometime between the thirteenth and the tenth century BC.